Dear Parent:

Congratulations! Your child is taking the first steps on an exciting journey. The destination? Independent reading!

STEP INTO READING® will help your child get there. The program offers five steps to reading success. Each step includes fun stories and colorful art. There are also Step into Reading Sticker Books, Step into Reading Math Readers, Step into Reading Write-In Readers, Step into Reading Phonics Readers, and Step into Reading Phonics First Steps! Boxed Sets—a complete literacy program with something for every child.

Learning to Read, Step by Step!

Ready to Read   Preschool–Kindergarten
• big type and easy words • rhyme and rhythm • picture clues
For children who know the alphabet and are eager to begin reading.

Reading with Help   Preschool–Grade 1
• basic vocabulary • short sentences • simple stories
For children who recognize familiar words and sound out new words with help.

Reading on Your Own   Grades 1–3
• engaging characters • easy-to-follow plots • popular topics
For children who are ready to read on their own.

Reading Paragraphs   Grades 2–3
• challenging vocabulary • short paragraphs • exciting stories
For newly independent readers who read simple sentences with confidence.

Ready for Chapters   Grades 2–4
• chapters • longer paragraphs • full-color art
For children who want to take the plunge into chapter books but still like colorful pictures.

STEP INTO READING® is designed to give every child a successful reading experience. The grade levels are only guides. Children can progress through the steps at their own speed, developing confidence in their reading, no matter what their grade.

Remember, a lifetime love of reading starts with a single step!

For Charlie and Allison—D.M.R.
For Dad and Sherry—M.I.

With grateful acknowledgment to Frank Lange for his time and expertise in reviewing this book.

Text copyright © 2009 by Dana Meachen Rau
Illustrations copyright © 2009 by Melissa Iwai

Visit us on the Web!
www.stepintoreading.com

Educators and librarians, for a variety of teaching tools, visit us at
www.randomhouse.com/teachers

Library of Congress Cataloging-in-Publication Data
Rau, Dana Meachen.
Corn aplenty / by Dana Meachen Rau ; illustrated by Melissa Iwai. — 1st ed.
    p.   cm. — (Step into reading. A step 1 book)
Summary: Two children watch a local farmer grow a crop of corn and as the corn
develops—from seed to harvest time—so does the friendship between the children and
the farmer.
ISBN 978-0-375-85575-7 (pbk.) — ISBN 978-0-375-95575-4 (lib. bdg.)
[1. Farmers—Fiction. 2. Corn—Fiction. 3. Friendship—Fiction.] I. Iwai, Melissa, ill. II. Title.
PZ7.R193975Co 2009
[E]—dc22   2008009716

Printed in the United States of America

10 9 8 7 6 5 4 3

First Edition

STEP INTO READING® STEP 1

Corn Aplenty

by Dana Meachen Rau

illustrated by Melissa Iwai

Random House 🏠 New York

We drive by a farm.

The farmer
plows the field.

The dirt is
brown and bumpy.

We ride by the farm.

The farmer
plants the seeds.

The seeds are
yellow and small.

We skip by the farm.

The farmer
feeds the plants.

The seedlings are
green and soft.

We stop by the farm.

The farmer
waters the plants.

The stalks are
strong and tall.

We race to the farm.

The farmer
picks the corn.

The bins are
full and heavy.

We walk
to the farm stand.

The farmer
sells his corn.

The ears are
big and plump.

We help count.

We help carry.

The farmer thanks us
with plenty of corn.

We thank him
with dinner!